SWEET ASSURANCE

26 Gospel Arrangements for Ladies' Choir or Ensemble

◆ BY MOSIE LISTER ◆

Lillenas Publishing Co.
KANSAS CITY, MO. 64141

◆ CONTENTS ◆

I Go to the Rock

DOTTIE RAMBO
Arr. by Mosie Lister

1. Where do I go _____ when there's
2. Where do I hide _____ till the

no one else ____ to turn to? Who do I talk to _____
storms have all ____ passed o - ver? Where do I run to _____

The King of Who I Am

T. G. & M. S.

TANYA GOODMAN
MICHAEL SYKES
Arr. by Mosie Lister

are my king,_____ You are the Lamb,_____ Li - on of Ju - dah, Seed of A - bra - ham;_____ The Ho - ly One,_____ God's on - ly Son, You are the king of who I am. You

12

How Long Has It Been?

M. L.

MOSIE LISTER

Intently ♩ = 76

1. How long has it been since you talked with the Lord And told Him your heart's hid-den se - crets?_____ How long since you prayed? How long since you stayed On your

knew that He cared for you?

2. How long has it been since you knelt by your bed And prayed to the Lord up in heav-en?_____ How long since you knew that He'd an-swer you And would

18

When They Call My Name

M. L.

MOSIE LISTER

Holy Spirit, Thou Art Welcome

D. R.

DOTTIE RAMBO and DAVID HUNTSINGER
Arr. by Joseph Linn
SSA arr. by Mosie Lister

mer - cy___ and grace,___ Thou art wel - come in_____ this

place._____ Oo_____

Lord, in Thy pres -ence_____ there's heal - ing di - vine;

No oth-er pow - er can save, Lord, but Thine._____ Ho-ly

28

*Instrumental track continues. If a capella option is desired, tape operator should fade tracks.

A New Name in Glory

C. A. M.

C. AUSTIN MILES
Arr. by Mosie Lister

30

new name writ-ten down in glo - ry; And it's mine,_____ oh, yes, it's

mine. And the white - robed an - gels sing the sto - ry,_____ "A

sin - ner has come home."_____ There's a new name writ-ten down in

glo - ry, And it's mine;_____ oh, yes, it's mine. With my

That my name was writ - ten down, writ-ten down. There's a

new name writ-ten down in glo-ry;___ And it's mine, oh, yes, it's mine.___

___ And the white - robed an-gels sing the sto-ry,___ "A sin - ner has come

home, has come home." There's a new name writ-ten down in

Love Through Me

M. L.

MOSIE LISTER

The Eastern Gate

I. G. M.

Arr. by I. G. Martin
and Mosie Lister

Enthusiastically ♩ = 72

I will meet you in the morn - ing, Just in - side the East-ern Gate. Then be read - y, faith - ful

38

39

Sweet Will of God

L. N. M.

LELIA N. MORRIS
Arr. by Mosie Lister

1. My stub-born will at last___ has___ yield-ed; I would be
Thee, oh, Lord,___ for - ev - er, My way-ward

Thine, and Thine___ a - lone. But this the prayer___ my lips are
feet no more___ to___ roam; What pow'r from Thee___ my soul can

bring - ing, "Lord, let in me Thy will___ be___ done." Sweet
sev - er? The cen - ter of God's will___ my___ home.

I've Been Changed

M. L.

MOSIE LISTER

46

47

A Storm Now and Then

M. L.

MOSIE LISTER

1. All my dreams were shat-tered, and___ all that mat-tered Was
   feet are stum-bling and my hopes are crum-bling, The

gone___ on the winds of sor - row. Ev - 'ry - thing___ I had
Lord___ is there a - bid - ing. There is peace,___ there is

planned swept___ out___ of my hand And I saw no hope for to -
calm in the midst___ of the storm; The___ Lord is there a -

50

Jesus Is Coming Soon

R. E. W.

R. E. WINSETT
Arr. by Joseph Linn
SSA arr. by Mosie Lister

1. Trou-ble-some times are here, fill-ing men's hearts with fear;
Free-dom we all hold dear now is at stake.____

man - y cold, los - ing their homes of gold;
This in God's Word is told, e - vils a - bound.____

56

Wonderful Savior

J. D. S.

J. D. SUMNER
Arr. by Joseph Linn
SSA arr. by Mosie Lister

Come and Dine

C. B. W.

C. B. WIDMEYER
Arr. by Mosie Lister

1. Je - sus has a ta - ble spread Where the saints of God are fed; He in -
2. The dis - ci - ples came to land, Thus o - bey-ing Christ's com-mand; For the

vites His cho - sen peo - ple, "Come and dine." With His man - na He doth
Mas - ter called to them, "Oh, come and dine." There they found their heart's de -

feed And sup - plies our ev - 'ry need. Oh, 'tis sweet to sup with Je - sus all the
sire, Bread and fish up - on the fire; Thus He sat - is - fies the hun - gry ev - 'ry

I'd Rather Have Jesus

RHEA F. MILLER

GEORGE BEVERLY SHEA
Arr. by Mosie Lister

2nd time to Coda

Dwelling in Beulah Land

C. A. M.

C. AUSTIN MILES
Arr. by Mosie Lister

1. Far a-way the noise of strife up-on my ear is fall-ing; Then I know the sins of earth be-set on ev-'ry hand._____ Doubt and fear and things of earth in

feast-ing on the man-na from a boun-ti-ful sup-

ply, For I am dwell-ing in Beu-lah land.

2. View-ing here the works of God I

74

I Don't Need to Understand

M. C.

MAGDALENE CROCKER
Arr. by Mosie Lister

1. Sun-shine comes and sun-shine goes, then shad-ows lin-ger; Dark - ness fills the night with mys - te - ry and care. But with - in my heart a gen - tle voice re - minds me,

From the First Hallelujah to the Last Amen

D. B.

DAVE BOLLING
Arr. by Stan Pethel
SSA arr. by Mosie Lister

1. Of - ten in a rev - 'rent time we say a - men; And when our hearts are
2. We say "hal - le - lu - jah"; that means, praise the Lord. And "a - men" sim - ply

joy - ful, hal - le - lu - jahs ring a - gain. In old camp-meet-ings on the grass or
tells us that our hearts are in ac - cord. So if you feel re - strict - ed, strike a

tem - ples built by men, A saint shouts hal - le - lu - jah and we all join
brand_ new_ chord; Let's all a - gree to - geth - er now to praise the

86

'Til the Storm Passes By

M. L.

MOSIE LISTER
Arr. by Rick Powell
SSA arr. by M. L.

1. In the dark of the mid-night have I oft hid my face, While the storm howls a-bove me and there's no hid-ing place. 'Mid the crash of the thun-der, pre-cious Lord, hear my cry; Keep me safe 'til the

I Won't Turn Back

M. L.

MOSIE LISTER
Arr. by Joseph Linn
SSA arr. by Mosie Lister

92

94

While Ages Roll

M. L.

MOSIE LISTER

Warmly, not too slow ♩ = 92

1. Some

day this stam-m'ring tongue will fal - ter no more
mil - lion years have passed in that won - der - ful place,

And a grand - er, sweet-er song I shall sing;
My song of praise will just have be - gun;

voice will nev-er tire or grow___ old;_____ And my

song shall ev-er be, "Praise the Lamb who died for me"; And I'll

sing it while a - ges shall roll._____ I'll

sing it while a - ges shall roll._____

All Because of God's Amazing Grace

S. W. A.

STEPHEN W. ADAMS
Arr. by Mosie Lister

105

Alleluia to the King

M. L.

MOSIE LISTER

Worshipfully

1. Be - cause God is ho - ly I will bow down be - fore__ Him. Be - cause He is ho - ly,_____ His name I a - dore. Be - cause God is wor - thy,

108

Come and See the Man
(at the Well)

M. L.

MOSIE LISTER

1. To - day I met a Man at the well
2. He told me a-bout a well that won't run dry,

Who told me a-bout a dif - f'rent kind of
And then He talked a-bout the heav'n - ly

114

Led by the Master's Hand

M. L.

MOSIE LISTER

Lyrics:
1. As I walk the road of life my feet grow wea-ry,_____ And I stum-ble through the thorns and shift-ing sand._____ But I

118

120

At the Right Time

M. L.

MOSIE LISTER